P9-APY-081

The 2002
Commemorative
Stamp Yearbook

United States Postal Service

Other books available from
the United States Postal Service:

An American Postal Portrait

The 2001 Commemorative Stamp Yearbook

The Postal Service Guide to U.S. Stamps
Twenty-Eighth Edition
Twenty-Ninth Edition

HarperResource
An Imprint of HarperCollins Publishers

The 2002 Commemorative Stamp Yearbook

United States Postal Service

UNITED STATES POSTAL SERVICE ®

HarperResource
An Imprint of HarperCollinsPublishers

2002 COMMEMORATIVE STAMP YEARBOOK:
Copyright © 2002 by the United States Postal Service.
All rights reserved. Printed in the United States of America.
No part of this book may be used or reproduced in any manner
whatsoever without written permission except in the case of
brief quotations embodied in critical articles and reviews.
For information address HarperCollins Publishers Inc.,
10 East 53rd Street, New York, NY 10022.

The designs of stamps and postal stationery are the subject of individual
copyrights by the United States Postal Service. UNITED STATES POSTAL
SERVICE, the eagle logo, and POSTAL SERVICE are trademarks
of the United States Postal Service.

HarperCollins books may be purchased for educational,
business, or sales promotional use. For information please write:
Special Markets Department, HarperCollins Publishers Inc.,
10 East 53rd Street, New York, NY 10022.

Library of Congress Cataloging-in-Publication Data has been applied for.
ISBN: 0-06-019898-2

Contents

Greetings From America

From the halls of the United States Military Academy to the sand and surf at Waikiki Beach in Hawaii, this year's commemorative stamps offer a grand tour of the best of America—with some of the country's finest artistic talents serving as expert guides.

At the heart of the 2002 program is Greetings From America, the first pane of 50 stamps in a decade. These colorful stamps pay tribute to the unique American landscape with nostalgic designs reminiscent of the retro "large letter" postcards inspired by decades of travel and adventure. With their lively illustrations of picturesque monuments and landmarks, each of these stamps tells a story. And this year, the people behind the stamps have stories to tell, too.

Did you know that the designer of the Duke Kahanamoku stamp is a lifelong surfer? Or that the photographs on the American Bats stamps were shot by one of the world's leading bat experts—who also happens to be one of the world's leading bat photographers? This new edition of the *Commemorative Stamp Yearbook* offers a behind-the-scenes look at the 2002 stamp program. In their own words, U.S. Postal Service designers, art directors, photographers, illustrators, and consultants talk about the challenges of creating a commemorative stamp, whether they're photographing a five-foot military crest for reduction to stamp size or painting a complex American ecosystem teeming with plant and animal life.

Read on to learn more about these talented individuals and their contributions to the 2002 stamp program. As these intriguing new stamps travel around the nation and throughout the world, not everyone will be aware of the fascinating stories behind them. But the message they send will be absolutely clear: "Greetings From America!"

Year of the Horse

When the U.S. Postal Service needed a designer for its Year of the Rooster stamp in 1992, award-winning graphic artist Clarence Lee of Honolulu, Hawaii, was the clear choice. When the stamp proved to be extremely popular, Lee was asked to design all of the subsequent Lunar New Year stamps, beautifully sustaining his original design concept throughout the entire series.

To commemorate the Year of the Horse, which began on February 12, 2002, Lee created an intricate paper-cut design of a horse, the seventh of twelve animals associated with the Chinese lunar calendar. He then incorporated Chinese characters reading "Year of the Horse" in grass-style calligraphy by Lau Bun, a respected calligrapher from a family of prominent Chinese calligraphers.

According to Lee, using paper-cut designs was a natural choice for this stamp series. "Through our research, we discovered that the art of paper-cutting images had a long tradition in China," he explains. "The people in the countryside with very few resources would revert to cutting paper as a means of artistic expression. They would put them in their homes, on doorways, and on windows, and would give them as gifts to each other. Our design was an attempt to respect and recognize the cultural heritage of this old art form. It became a pleasant challenge to depict all the lunar animals with this traditional technique."

Lee also points out that working on the Lunar New Year stamps gave him an opportunity not only to learn about his own heritage, but also to contemplate the lives that his ancestors gave up in their homeland in order to come to America.

"We all have stories of our courageous immigrants who came from all over the world to make a better life for their future families," he says. "It was an honor to have been part of a stamp that honors not only Chinese but all Americans who have come to this great country."

FACING PAGE: This 18th-century painting, now in the Musée Guimet in Paris, depicts the voyage of Emperor Qianlong.

New York, NY
February 11, 2002
Place and Date of Issue

Clarence Lee
Artist, Designer

Terrence W. McCaffrey
Art Director

BLACK HERITAGE

USA 34

Langston Hughes

Langston Hughes

"If one may ascribe a prime function to any creative writing, it is I think, to affirm life, to yea-say the excitement of living in rela- tion to the vast rhythms of the universe of which we are a part, to untie the riddles of the gutter in order to closer tie the knot between man and God."

— *Langston Hughes*

Shortly before his death in 1967, Langston Hughes was asked for a one-sentence description of his life's work for inclusion in *Who's Who in America*. His response was simple, elegant, and characteristically ambitious. "My seek- ing has been to explain and illuminate the Negro condition in America," he wrote, "and obliquely that of all human kind."

Born in Joplin, Missouri, in 1902, James Langston Hughes is considered one of the most important American writers of the 20th century. When he was only 19, his poem "The Negro Speaks of Rivers" was published in the June 1921 issue of *The Crisis*, the jour- nal of the NAACP. His first book of poetry, *The Weary Blues*, was published in 1926, three years before he graduated from Lincoln University.

Although he considered himself a poet first, Hughes wrote in a wide range of literary genres. During the 1930s his poetry and plays confronted not only the economic impact of the Great Depression on African Americans, but also the devas- tating consequences of ongoing racial injustice. In the 1940s he created his popular character Jesse B. Semple—nicknamed Simple—who appeared in the newspaper column Hughes wrote for the *Chicago Defender*. Hughes collected the "Simple" columns in five books and also made him the central character in a musical play.

During the 1950s and 1960s Hughes wrote books for children and young adults on such topics as Africa, the Caribbean, famous African Americans, and jazz. He edited anthologies of black poetry,

New York, NY
February 1, 2002
Place and Date of Issue

Henri Cartier-Bresson
Photographer

Richard Sheaff
Designer, Art Director

short stories, and folklore, bringing the rich- ness of black culture to readers of all races.

This 25th stamp in the Black Heritage series honors Hughes on the centennial of his birth with a photograph by Henri Cartier-Bresson. The French photographer and the American writer were good friends, and during a winter in Mexico in the 1930s they shared an apartment.

"He was a noble human being," Cartier-Bresson later remi- nisced to Hughes' biographer Arnold Rampersad. "But he was also natural, always smiling, always good-humored, even if you could sense that he kept something in reserve." The pho- tographer's affection for his friend, as well as Hughes' warm demeanor, are readily apparent in this photograph. But deter- mining when the photograph had been taken proved tricky, since it had been assigned various dates over the years. The problem was solved by looking at Cartier-Bresson's log and the original contact sheet for the photo shoot, which indicated that the year was most likely 1946.

FACING PAGE: A pastel of Hughes by Winold Reiss. ABOVE: A 1939 photo of Hughes by Carl Van Vechten. CENTER: Hughes' first book of poetry, The Weary Blues, *was published in 1926.*

Winter Sports

The cold temperatures and snowy conditions that keep many inside during the winter are essential for athletes who take part in winter sports. This year the U.S. Postal Service recognizes the competitive drive of these athletes by issuing stamps depicting four popular winter sports: figure skating, ice hockey, snowboarding, and ski jumping.

Under the guidance of art director Phil Jordan, the firm of Jager Di Paola Kemp has taken a new direction in the art of stamp design. Each of the four Winter Sports stamps combines a photograph of an individual competitor with a graphic treatment of the corresponding sports arena or apparatus.

Representing a diverse group of winter sports presented a unique design challenge for everyone involved. "As the art director, I basically delineated the problem as I saw it," said Jordan, who describes his role in this project as a mediator between the Citizens' Stamp Advisory Committee and the design firm. "The firm came back with three different but all very interesting concepts, including one focusing heavily on photography. I showed all three to the committee and the design developed from there."

Superb examples of modern sports photography appear on the final stamp designs. Craig Melvin photographed the figure skater in 1998. The photograph of the ice hockey player was taken by David Madison in 1995. (Another of Madison's photographs appeared on the Summer Sports stamp issued in 2000.) Martin Tichy photographed the snowboarder—whose helmet was added electronically—in 2000, while Nancie Battaglia's 1998 photograph captured a ski jumper in mid-jump.

Park City, UT
January 8, 2002
Place and Date of Issue

Jager Di Paola Kemp
Designers

Phil Jordan
Art Director

36 U.S.C. Sec. 220506. Official Licensed Product of the United States Olympic Committee.

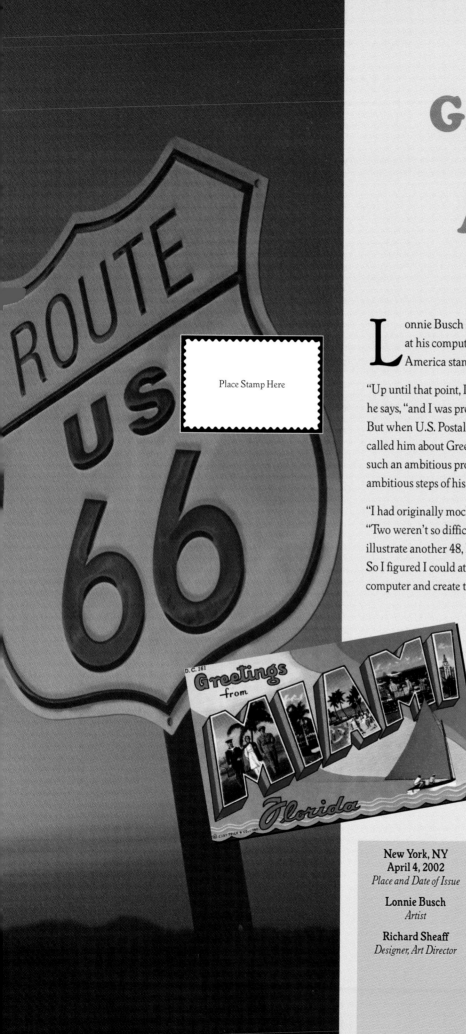

Place Stamp Here

Greetings From America

Lonnie Busch had only one problem when he sat down at his computer to illustrate the Greetings From America stamps: He had never used one before.

"Up until that point, I had done all of my artwork by airbrush," he says, "and I was pretty much against using a computer." But when U.S. Postal Service art director Richard Sheaff called him about Greetings From America, Busch knew that such an ambitious project required him to take some equally ambitious steps of his own.

"I had originally mocked up two of these stamps," he explains. "Two weren't so difficult—but when I realized I was about to illustrate another 48, I thought, 'How am I going to do this?' So I figured I could at least take care of the typesetting by computer and create the actual artwork traditionally."

But Busch was soon enamored with high technology, and within no time he was using his computer for more than just typesetting. "This project worked so well for me," he says with enthusiasm, "because it allowed me to learn how to master the computer for everything from layouts to scanning. It was quite a transition from my more traditional way of doing things."

Inspired by retro "large letter" post-cards that were used to advertise cities, states, or tourist attractions, Busch kept their bright colors and creative designs in mind as his own artwork began to take shape. Combining flora and fauna with

New York, NY
April 4, 2002
Place and Date of Issue

Lonnie Busch
Artist

Richard Sheaff
Designer, Art Director

local points of interest, he created colorful collages that celebrate the unique character of each state. The resulting works of art—which comprise the first pane of 50 stamps in 10 years—hint at the romance of travel and discovery and convey a nostalgia for all aspects of popular American culture.

A native of St. Louis, Missouri, Busch can be found these days in his studio in western North Carolina. Even after nearly 30 years as a designer and illustrator, he remains especially fond of the unique challenges of stamp design.

"I've worked with the Postal Service on quite a few projects," he says, citing his illustrations for a 1987 stamp commemorating the Pan-American Games, the 1991 Basketball Centennial stamp, a 1994 Love stamp, and stamps for the Winter Olympics in 1992 and 1994. But even with his experience creating small-scale, high-profile artwork, Busch laughs when he recalls the formidable task of representing all 50 states on a single pane. "They always give me so much freedom to do what I want, but this time it was a little daunting to get that much freedom!"

Of course, that creative freedom also allowed Busch to scour bookstores and libraries for his favorite images of each state's icons. In the process he learned a great deal about America's natural wonders, hidden corners, and unmistakable landmarks. "This project was so exciting and varied," he says, "and definitely full of surprises."

And what about his airbrush? To Lonnie Busch, its fate is the biggest surprise yet. "Within six months, I put it away—and I haven't used it since."

Harry Houdini

jacket escape. Houdini was bound in a straitjacket and a rope was tied around his ankles. He was then hoisted high above the crowd and suspended from a beam that projected from a window in a tall building.

Designer Richard Sheaff sorted through a wide range of visuals, including posters advertising Houdini's performances in Holland in 1903 and Germany in 1908, as well as a photograph on the cover of a souvenir program from his coast-to-coast U.S. tour in 1926 and 1927. Sheaff ultimately chose a portrait depicting a confident, self-assured Houdini at the height of his career, taken from a 1911 lithograph poster in the collection of Gary H. Mandelblatt of Westfield, New Jersey.

H arry Houdini astonished audiences with his daring escapes, not only from handcuffs but also from strait-jackets, ropes, chains, jail cells, even trunks submerged in water. His name is synonymous with magic and escape—but finding a way to capture such an elusive personality on a stamp required not only discussions with magic experts, museum curators, and private collectors, but also research into Houdini's fascinating life and career.

Harry Houdini was born Erich Weisz in Budapest, Hungary, on March 24, 1874. His family immigrated to the United States when he was four and settled first in Wisconsin. He went on to perform magic and escape tricks in dime museums, medicine shows, circuses, and other small venues, changing his name in the early 1890s as a tribute to the famous French illusionist, Jean-Eugene Robert Houdin. He began performing escape tricks on vaudeville stages in the spring of 1899, and by the following spring he had become the star known as the King of Handcuffs.

Beginning in 1915, he electrified audiences with his suspended strait-

"It's a very nice portrait of the man," says Sheaff, adding he wanted to find something other than the overused, iconic images of Houdini bound in chains or hanging upside down. "It's from a rare poster, so it probably isn't a picture that most people have already seen."

TOP: Houdini in a typical predicament, c.1899. CENTER AND BELOW: Advertisements for Houdini's performances. FACING PAGE: A 1908 poster shows Houdini being manacled by the Berlin police.

New York, NY
July 3, 2002
Place and Date of Issue

Richard Sheaff
Designer, Art Director

Happy Birthday

Stamps are meant to commemorate both special events and special people. Put this new Happy Birthday stamp on cards and packages and you'll be doing both—while adding a festive touch that will delight family and friends.

Like the two previous Happy Birthday stamps, which were issued in Special Occasions booklets in 1987 and 1988, this 2002 stamp recognizes the tradition of sending special birthday greetings and fulfills the mailing needs of the public at the same time.

"We continually receive requests for this stamp," notes Manager of Stamp Development Terrence W. McCaffrey, who also served as art director. "Unlike stamps celebrating an annual holiday, there's always a need for a year-round stamp to use on birthday cards. We found that while people liked the Special Occasions booklets, they wanted to be able to buy a Happy Birthday stamp without necessarily having to buy stamps for a variety of other occasions."

Designer Harry Zelenko created this colorful, celebratory design, which is sure to brighten envelopes throughout the year as Americans commemorate a friend or relative's "first day of issue."

Riverside, CA
February 8, 2002
Place and Date of Issue

Harry Zelenko
Designer

Terrence W. McCaffrey
Art Director

Neuter or Spay

The numbers are staggering: An estimated 70,000 cats and dogs are born each day in the United States. To combat the problem of animal overpopulation, animal shelters and veterinarians throughout the country urge pet owners to neuter or spay their dogs and cats.

Neutering or spaying simply makes sense, since these procedures can lead to better health and longer lives. For example, neutered male dogs and cats have a decreased chance of developing prostate disease and are also less likely to stray from home. Among female cats and dogs, spaying decreases the rate of breast cancer and eliminates nervous behavior associated with the heat cycle.

To find the perfect visuals for these stamps, photographer Sally Andersen-Bruce visited several no-kill shelters near her home in Connecticut before choosing to focus on a mixed-breed kitten and a mixed-breed puppy. Andersen-Bruce says the two young animals — who were respectively neutered and spayed according to the shelters' policies — greatly enjoyed posing for the camera.

"The kitten was a very affectionate model," she says. "She would cock her head to the right, then to the left, and look straight into the lens of the camera. You couldn't help but fall in love with her."

Andersen-Bruce is pleased to report that the kitten made a lifetime friend during the photo shoot. "While I was photographing her a little girl named Hanna peeked around the corner. She and her family adopted the kitten and promptly gave her a good home."

The puppy also found a loving home with an adoptive family that includes two teenagers and a ten-year-old golden retriever. "The fourteen-year-old son wanted a second dog," says Andersen-Bruce, "and he insisted that the dog had to come from a shelter. "

Assisting during the photo shoot was a high school student named Brianna. "She loves puppies and kittens but her mom won't let her have one right now," Andersen-Bruce explains, "so her job was to hug the kittens and puppies and hold them up for the camera." In addition to learning about the importance of spaying and neutering pets, Brianna also discovered a new interest: She is now studying photography in school.

Denver, CO
September 20, 2002
Place and Date of Issue

Sally Andersen-Bruce
Photographer

Derry Noyes
Designer, Art Director

Ogden Nash

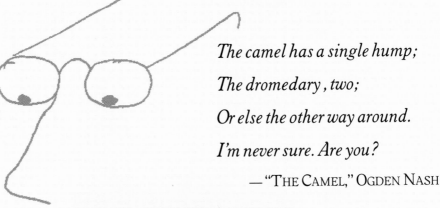

The camel has a single hump;
The dromedary , two;
Or else the other way around.
I'm never sure. Are you?

— "THE CAMEL," OGDEN NASH

"I'm very fond of the English language," Odgen Nash reportedly said. "I tease it, and you tease only the things you love." A gentle satirist, Nash poked fun at human foibles without cynicism. He wrote on many subjects, but all of his poems expressed his wry wit and demonstrated his playfulness with language. He invented words and used puns, creative misspellings, irregular line lengths, and unexpected rhymes to make his verse humorous and memorable, so it's no wonder that many consider him to have been one of the most accomplished American writers of light verse in the 20th century.

But what color were his eyes?

Michael J. Deas, who has illustrated five other stamps in the Literary Arts series, needed to know. For this stamp honoring Nash on the centennial of his birth in 1902, Deas based his portrait on a circa 1952 photograph taken by Kay Bell Reynal, a fashion photographer whose subjects included prominent writers and artists. Reynal's photograph was charming, but since it was black and white it provided few clues about which colors were appropriate for the stamp. The question was best answered by those who knew Ogden Nash best.

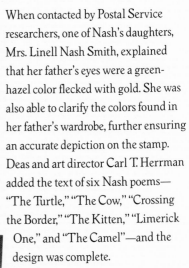

When contacted by Postal Service researchers, one of Nash's daughters, Mrs. Linell Nash Smith, explained that her father's eyes were a green-hazel color flecked with gold. She was also able to clarify the colors found in her father's wardrobe, further ensuring an accurate depiction on the stamp. Deas and art director Carl T. Herrman added the text of six Nash poems— "The Turtle," "The Cow," "Crossing the Border," "The Kitten," "Limerick One," and "The Camel"—and the design was complete.

Thorough research turned up another amusing tidbit. In a letter to the editor of the *New York Times,* published December 29, 1969, Ogden Nash complained about stamps that would not stick to envelopes. He lamented, "The Post Office should supply a roll of Scotch tape with every 100 stamps, but mine won't even sell me one. I'd like to go back to where I came from: 1902." Ogden Nash might be pleased to know that in 2002 the self-adhesive stamps bearing his likeness will indeed stick to envelopes.

Baltimore, MD
August 19, 2002
Place and Date of Issue

Michael J. Deas
Artist

Carl T. Herrman
Designer, Art Director

TOP: A doodle by Nash. CENTER: Nash was the recipient of several honorary degrees. BOTTOM: Nash's poem "Invocation" was published in the January 11, 1930, issue of The New Yorker. *FACING PAGE: Nash in 1953.*

The turtle lives 'twixt plated decks

Which practically conceal its sex.

I think it clever of the turtle

In such a fix to be so fertile.

—"The Turtle," Ogden Nash

Masters of American Photography

When Derry Noyes learned that she was going to serve as designer and art director for the Masters of American Photography stamp pane, she couldn't wait to delve into the research and design process. "I've always loved black-and-white photography," says Noyes, "so I was thrilled to be working on this project."

In consultation with Peter C. Bunnell, a faculty curator at The Art Museum at Princeton University and a noted authority on American photography, Noyes selected photographers and their work with an awareness that the images they chose had a specific story to tell. "We were locked into a chronology, but that was important," she explains. "The stamp pane serves not only as a history of the art of photography in America, but also as a capsule history of our country."

The daguerreotype process was announced and demonstrated in the United States in 1839. Named for its French inventor, Louis Jacques Mandé Daguerre, a daguerreotype was made by fixing an image onto a silver-plated, chemically treated sheet of copper. That same year in England, William Henry Fox Talbot announced the creation of a process he called photogenic drawing, which fixed images directly onto sheets of chemically treated paper, producing both negative and positive pictures. Photographic technology progressed rapidly and Americans enthusiastically embraced the new medium, using the camera for myriad purposes.

ABOVE: James VanDerZee's 1918 self-portrait. CENTER: Paul Strand photographed by Alfred Stieglitz in 1917. BACKGROUND: W. Eugene Smith, Pittsburgh, c. 1955, by Fran Erzen.

San Diego, CA
June 13, 2002
Place and Date of Issue

Derry Noyes
Designer, Art Director

MASTERS OF
American Photography

 Lewis W. Hine 1874–1940

 Edward Weston 1886–1958

 Paul Strand 1890–1976

 Minor White 1908–1976

Gertrude Käsebier 1852–1934

Man Ray 1890–1976

W. Eugene Smith 1918–1978

Garry Winogrand 1928–1984

Carleton E. Watkins 1829–1916

Alfred Stieglitz 1864–1946

Walker Evans 1903–1975

André Kertész 1894–1985

Timothy H. O'Sullivan 1840–1882

Edward Steichen 1879–1973

Dorothea Lange 1895–1965

Imogen Cunningham 1883–1976

Southworth 1811–1894 Hawes 1808–1901

Alvin Langdon Coburn 1882–1966

James VanDerZee 1886–1983

Ansel Adams 1902–1984

PLATE POSITION

20 x .37 = $7.40

© 2001 USPS

S111

S111

"To record and interpret these qualities for others, to brighten the drab moods of cities,
and build high horizons of the spirit on the edge of plain and desert—
these are some of the many obligations of art."
— ANSEL ADAMS

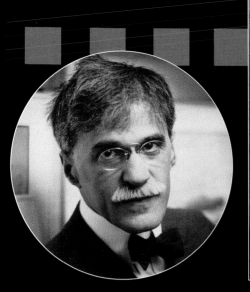

For example, renowned art photographer Ansel Adams was praised for his sublime interpretations of the dramatic beauty found in the western landscape. Rendered with a naturalist's precision and a pictorialist's virtuosity, his works reveal a sharpness of detail and a rich tonal range that are hallmarks of his style. Other photographers such as Man Ray, an artist who worked in all media, expanded the limits of photography itself. One of his innovations was the creation of cameraless images he called rayographs, made by placing objects on photographic paper and exposing the arrangement to light.

An inquisitive look into the background of each photograph led to some interesting discoveries. For example, the identity of the World War II soldier in the W. Eugene Smith photograph on this stamp pane was hazy until U.S. Postal Service legal researchers talked to a curator at a photography archive in Tucson, Arizona. She was able to identify the marine in the photograph after she happened, simply by chance, to see a picture from the same shoot in a restaurant called Evangelo's in Santa Fe, New Mexico. As it turned out, not only was the restaurant named for the marine, Evangelo Klonis, but it was also owned by his son Nick.

When the U.S. Postal Service contacted Nick Klonis, he was thrilled to hear about the stamp. He told researchers that he's the spitting image of his father—and that he's looking forward to hanging a copy of the stamp in the restaurant.

Not surprisingly, Noyes designed the Masters of American Photography stamp pane with just that sort of intention in mind.

"As you take each stamp off the pane, it should feel like a picture in a frame," she says, explaining that she tried a wide range of formats and adjusted the borders until she achieved the desired effect. Noyes is satisfied with the end result: "It took a great deal of trial and error and experimenting with different formats," she says of the design process, "but these powerful photographs have become extremely powerful stamps."

FACING PAGE: Ansel Adams adjusting a camera in 1966. ABOVE (left to right): Alfred Stieglitz in a 1915 photograph by Edward Steichen; Imogen Cunningham's Self-portrait with Camera, *from the late 1920s; Walker Evans in the 1940s or 1950s. BELOW (left to right): Alvin Langdon Coburn at work, c. 1900; Edward Steichen on an aircraft carrier during World War II; Dorothea Lange, c.1934.*

United States Military Academy

a military academy at West Point, the United States Military Academy has prepared each graduate for a career as an officer in the U.S. Army and a lifetime of selfless service to the nation.

Today the academy is a fully diversified multicultural environment where future leaders see how to learn from and work with people from every corner of the nation. The academy is both proud of the record of its past graduates and confident that the same excellence will be achieved by the more than 4,000 young men and women who comprise its Corps of Cadets today.

For this stamp, the honor of capturing the perfect image to commemorate the academy's bicentennial fell to Ted Spiegel, a meticulous photographer who spent 25 years on assignment for the National Geographic Society. Intent on creating an "eye-biting image," Spiegel faced an interesting photographic challenge when he visited the United States Military Academy on a sunny summer day.

"The crest is in the middle of the Visitors Center," Spiegel explains, "so I coordinated to take the photos of the crest at high noon—which in the summertime was actually one o'clock—when I knew that the clerestory windows would allow for the maximum amount of sunlight. I arranged for them to turn off the lights to prevent any fluorescent light so that I could make a 20-second exposure. I basically used the interior as a huge light tent."

George Washington knew that West Point was the key to the continent—holding it prevented the British from gaining control of the vital Hudson River Valley and dividing the colonies in two. Today West Point is the key to American leadership; its many graduates have included Robert E. Lee, Ulysses S. Grant, Dwight D. Eisenhower, and H. Norman Schwarzkopf. Since President Thomas Jefferson signed legislation in 1802 establishing

TOP: The academy's Cadet Color Guard. RIGHT: Washington Hall with the Cadet Chapel in background. FACING PAGE: West Point graduates celebrate their accomplishments.

West Point, NY
March 16, 2002
Place and Date of Issue

Ted Spiegel
Photographer

Derry Noyes
Designer, Art Director

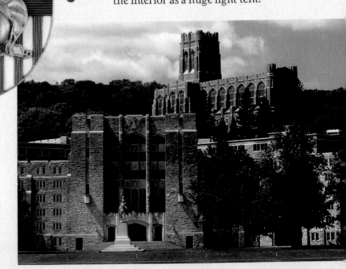

Cary Grant

Sometimes a stamp artist gets immersed in his subject. Just ask Michael J. Deas: He sees reminders of Cary Grant whenever he walks down the street.

"My favorite Cary Grant movie," says Deas, "is *Arsenic and Old Lace*, because it's set in my neighborhood in Brooklyn. Sometimes as I walk around, I like to pick out houses that I surmise may have inspired the film."

As an ardent film buff, Deas was quite interested in working on the Cary Grant stamp. "I've always been a big fan of Cary Grant, and I've worked on several previous Legends of Hollywood stamps, so I was hoping they'd tap me to do this one."

For this eighth Legends of Hollywood stamp, Deas and art director Carl T. Herrman were faced with the challenge of

creating a single image to exemplify the legendary actor. But with his eye for detail, Deas couldn't fail to notice that he had to decide *which* Cary Grant to depict.

"From the 1930s, when he acted alongside stars such as Mae West, until the 1960s, there were actually several stages in his process of maturing," Deas explains. "He looked distinctively different at each stage. And then there was another dilemma: whether to show him in a light-comedy persona, or as more of a leading man." In the end, Deas and Herrman decided to depict an elegant, formal Cary Grant in what Deas calls the actor's "middle period," around the mid-1950s.

Deas still marvels at Grant's enduring charm, and he adds that the actor would have been a handsome artistic subject regardless of when the stamp art portrayed him.

"He seemed to get better looking with age," says Deas. "He didn't so much defy the laws of aging as stand them on their ear."

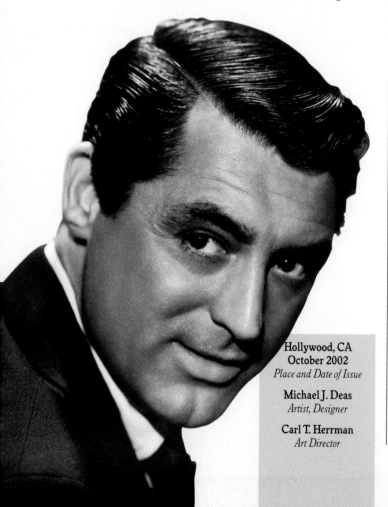

Hollywood, CA
October 2002
Place and Date of Issue

Michael J. Deas
Artist, Designer

Carl T. Herrman
Art Director

ABOVE: Grant with Katharine Hepburn in The Philadelphia Story, *1940. LEFT: Grant brought wit and sophistication to his varied roles in more than 70 movies. FACING PAGE: Cary Grant starred with Ingrid Bergman in the 1946 film* Notorious.

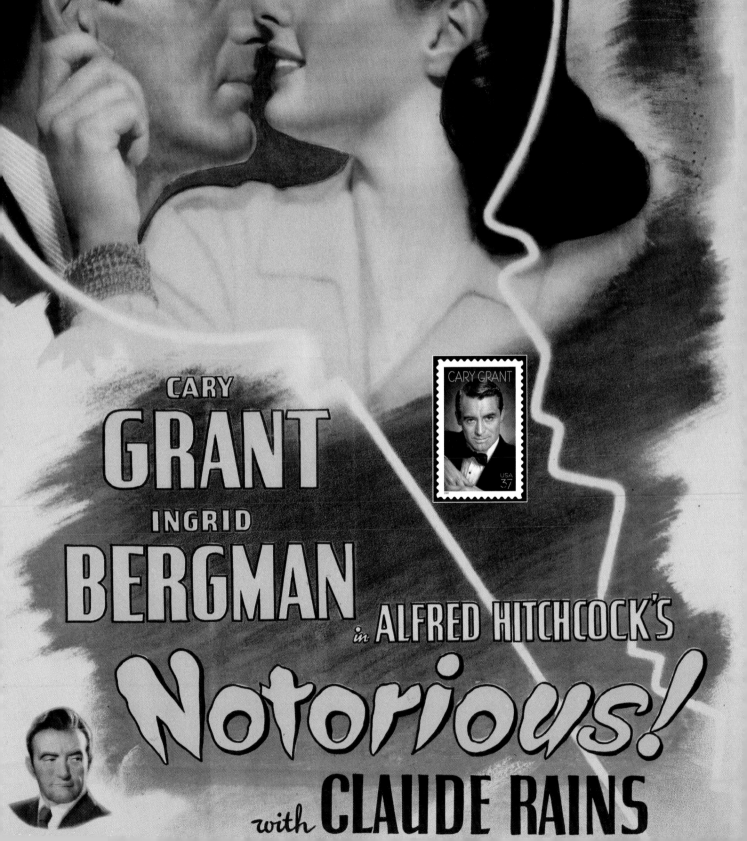

Mentoring a Child

With the issuance of the Mentoring a Child stamp, the U.S. Postal Service continues its tradition of raising public awareness of social issues. Today many young people lack positive adult role models, and mentors—dedicated volunteers who offer friendship, guidance, and support to youth—can fill this need.

But how does an artist convey the essence of an abstract subject like mentoring? According to Lance Hidy, the

respected poster artist who illustrated and designed the Mentoring a Child stamp, the process is one of research, trial and error, and inspiration.

Hidy began by brainstorming with art director Derry Noyes. "Derry sent an article about why the federal Office of Juvenile Justice and Delinquency Prevention has become so enthusiastic about mentoring," he explains. "She underlined these key passages: 'one-to-one relationship between a pair of unrelated individuals, usually of different ages . . . supports, teaches, counsels, and assists another . . . caring support and guidance . . . nurturing . . . friend, role model, guide, and teacher of values.'"

Hidy then began studying the artwork and photographs appearing in literature about mentoring as he searched for

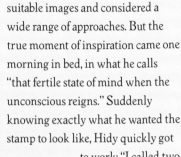

suitable images and considered a wide range of approaches. But the true moment of inspiration came one morning in bed, in what he calls "that fertile state of mind when the unconscious reigns." Suddenly knowing exactly what he wanted the stamp to look like, Hidy quickly got to work: "I called two sets of models, shot six rolls of film, and got one photograph that was perfect."

For the Mentoring a Child stamp, Hidy used photographs as reference for pencil-and-ink drawings that formed the basis for his final, computer-generated design. Even the font was carefully chosen. Known as Penumbra, it was designed for Adobe Systems in 1994 by Hidy himself, who intended to combine "the look of classical stone inscriptions with a contemporary feeling." The result is a stamp that not only recognizes the importance of mentors, but also invites Americans to share their values, goals, and skills with children whose lives can be forever changed by a responsible, caring adult.

Annapolis, MD
January 10, 2002
Place and Date of Issue

Lance Hidy
Artist, Designer

Derry Noyes
Art Director

MENTORING A CHILD

VALUES · GOALS · SKILLS

Tallahassee, FL
April 26, 2002
Place and Date of Issue

John D. Dawson
Artist

Ethel Kessler
Designer, Art Director

Longleaf Pine Forest

W hen artist John D. Dawson learned that Longleaf Pine Forest would be the fourth pane in the Nature of America series, he was reminded of a trip that he and his wife, Kathleen, had taken several years earlier.

"We were with friends outside of Savannah, Georgia, looking for red-cockaded woodpeckers," he explains. "During our search, I was struck by the sparseness of the forest and so intrigued when we would come across these small, wet areas where pitcher plants, small orchids, and more were growing. All outdoor experiences are stored for possible future use!"

Dawson drew upon these experiences as he set out to create this stamp pane. He began with two black-and-white sketches that were reviewed by several scientists. He later developed a series of color paintings that he continued to modify as each version was scrutinized by experts and meticulously verified by researchers. "I don't have a problem with making changes in the art, as long as they are constructive and not just someone's whim," he says, praising everyone involved with the stamp development process. "This is a total team effort."

"John orchestrates the almost impossible," says Ethel Kessler, art director for the Nature of America series. She points out that the design considerations for such a complex pane of stamps can be especially challenging. "The astonishing thing about John's work," she says, "is that not only does the entire painting work as a wide view, but each and every stamp is a beauty unto itself."

Dawson's artwork did present one final design problem. Although 31 species of plant and animal life are depicted in the artwork, the size of the stamp pane allowed for identification of only 27 species on the back. Dawson and Kessler worked together to decide which species could be omitted from the numbered key and chose four: crane fly (*Tipula* sp.), wiregrass (*Aristida stricta*), oak toad (*Bufo quercicus*), and bracken fern (*Pteridium aquilinum*).

But for Dawson, one of the greatest thrills of working on the Nature of America series is being able to help people catch a glimpse of so many elusive plants and animals. "I never did get to see that woodpecker," he adds, "but I was happy to put one in this stamp pane."

Women in Journalism

For a U.S. Postal Service art director, finding the right artist for a stamp project can sometimes be a difficult task. But when he was asked to serve as art director for the Women in Journalism stamps, Howard E. Paine knew that collagist Fred Otnes was the perfect artist for the job. In fact, so did his fellow art directors during a meeting of the Citizens' Stamp Advisory Committee.

"Everyone said, 'Hey, that would be a good one for Fred Otnes,'" Paine recalls. Paine had worked with Otnes previously on the Pioneers of Communication stamps issued in 1996, so he was familiar with the artist's unique approach to creating collages. "Fred Otnes tends to do dark, mature grays and browns," he says, "and there's a density and a complexity to his artwork that's intriguing."

Working with clippings from books, magazines, and newspapers, Otnes constructed small collages representing an aspect of each journalist's career. He began with photographs, but that was only the first step. "The additional elements create atmosphere," he explains. "How the photo is used and how the surrounding space is occupied gives each piece of art its own identity."

The stamp honoring Nellie Bly (1864–1922) focuses on her sensationalistic and dangerous reporting for *The World*, a New York newspaper owned by Joseph Pulitzer. Bly—born Elizabeth Jane Cochran—wrote a number of reform-oriented exposés for *The World*, once even feigning insanity to gain admittance to an asylum to expose the poor treatment of patients. In 1889 she achieved widespread fame by traveling around the world in fewer than 80 days, to beat the record set by Jules Verne's fictional character Phileas Fogg.

LEFT: Nellie Bly in 1890.
FACING PAGE: Ida M. Tarbell in New York, c. 1904.

Ft. Worth, TX
September 14, 2002
Place and Date of Issue

Fred Otnes
Artist, Designer

Howard E. Paine
Art Director

HISTORY OF STANDARD OIL BY Ida M. Tarbell

McCLURE'S
MAGAZINE

NOVEMBER

The President and the General

For the stamp honoring Ida M. Tarbell (1857–1944), Otnes again chose elements that represent the reporter's most prominent professional connection. In 1894, Tarbell began writing for *McClure's Magazine.* Her most famous project was an exhaustive investigation of the Standard Oil Company and the methods that John D. Rockefeller, Sr., had used to consolidate his hold on the oil industry. Tarbell's detailed exposé—a series of articles published from 1902 to 1904—helped bring about legal actions that resulted in the breakup of Standard Oil several years later.

The journalism career of Ethel L. Payne (1911–1991) began rather unexpectedly while she was working at an Army Special Services club in Japan. She showed her journal to a visiting reporter from the *Chicago Defender*—an African-American paper with a national readership—and soon her observations about the experiences of African-American soldiers became the basis for front-page stories. In the early 1950s, Payne moved back to her hometown of Chicago to work full-time for the *Defender,* and two years later she took over the paper's one-person bureau in Washington, D.C. She covered key events in the civil rights movement and earned a reputation as an aggressive journalist willing to ask tough questions.

Marguerite Higgins (1920–1966) of the *New York Herald Tribune* was the first woman to win a Pulitzer Prize for international reporting. She covered World War II, the liberation of the Dachau concentration camp, the Nuremberg trials, and the Soviet Union's blockade of Berlin. She also repeatedly risked her life to cover the war in Korea.

Facing a mountain of photographs and clippings associated with these four trailblazing journalists, Otnes found himself modifying his usual approach—but only slightly. Doing justice to each subject simply meant that he had to reign in his penchant for detail. "As an artist, you'd always like to do more," he says, "but for something that will appear at the size of a stamp, the answer is actually to do a little less."

FACING PAGE: Marguerite Higgins at work in Korea in 1950. RIGHT: Ethel Payne in 1982.

WEATHER
PARTLY CLOUDY
Low   Near 20
High   Low 30s

DAILY DEFENDER 5¢

Chicago's Picture Newspaper

VOL. I—No. 9   CHICAGO, ILLINOIS—MONDAY, FEBRUARY 20, 1956   WANT ADS: CALL CA 5-5656

INDICT LAWYER IN BUS BOYCOTT

Probe Murder Of Dr. Brewer

American Bats

As dusk settles over Austin, Texas, locals know where to go for one of the country's most fascinating displays of nature in an urban setting: the Congress Avenue Bridge. From mid-March to early November, crowds gather as 1.5 million bats stir from their roosts beneath the bridge, forming several dark, swirling columns as they take to the early evening skies.

But when the bats first came to Austin, they were far from welcome. Engineers who reconstructed the downtown bridge in 1980 had no way of knowing that the new crevices beneath it would make ideal roosts. Some bats had already been living there, but when they began moving in by the thousands, Austin resounded with fearful calls for their eradication.

Fortunately, Dr. Merlin D. Tuttle, founder of Bat Conservation International (BCI), convinced the city that the bats were beneficial creatures worth saving rather than monsters to be feared. His efforts were so successful that BCI is now headquartered in Austin— and the Congress Avenue Bridge is not only a major tourist attraction, but also a source of local pride.

What Austin residents learned is that their bats eat approximately 10,000 to 30,000 pounds of insects each night. Throughout North America bats help balance populations of night-flying insects, from mosquitoes in our own backyards to pests that cost farmers billions of dollars annually. Bats also disperse seeds from fruits and are vital to the pollination of desert plants in the American Southwest.

Tuttle has been photographing bats for more than 20 years, ever since he was dismayed by too many photographs of snarling, defensive bats that inaccurately depicted their shy nature to an already suspicious public.

"So I began studying photography myself," he explains, "and soon discovered that people's negative attitudes about bats can be changed in minutes upon seeing how fascinating and beautiful bats can be." To create these stamps, designer Phil Jordan worked closely with Tuttle, sorting through his many bat photographs and becoming as familiar with the subject as possible.

The photographs on these striking stamps each represent Tuttle's incredible patience and an intimate understanding of bat behavior—not to mention his technical expertise with approximately 300 pounds of custom-built equipment.

Austin, TX
September 13, 2002
Place and Date of Issue

Merlin D. Tuttle
Photographer

Phil Jordan
Designer, Art Director

TOP: The short, broad wings of a leaf-nosed bat allow for great maneuverability. CENTER: A hoary bat mother with two young. FACING PAGE: Mexican free-tailed bats emerge from Frio Cave in Texas.

John James Audubon

"My business went on prosperously when I attended to it," wrote John James Audubon in 1828. "But birds were birds and my thoughts were ever and anon turning towards them as to my greatest delight. Beyond this, I really cared not. I seldom passed a day without drawing a bird or noting something respecting its habits."

Art director Derry Noyes chose Audubon's vividly colored and exquisitely rendered portrait of two species of tanager—"Louisiana Tanager" and "Scarlet Tanager"—for this second issuance in the American Treasures series. Inaugurated in 2001 with the Amish Quilts stamp pane, the series is intended to showcase beautiful works of American fine art and crafts.

John James Audubon (1785–1851) was a self-taught artist and naturalist whose magnum opus, *Birds of America*, has been described as "the finest pictorial ornithological book ever produced." Born in Saint-Domingue (now Haiti), Audubon was raised in France. He moved to the United States in 1803 and became a citizen a few years later.

By 1820, after a series of unsuccessful business enterprises, Audubon had dedicated himself to the project that became his life's work and greatest passion—a comprehensive survey of American birds, beautifully and realistically illustrated and shown in their natural habitats. The artwork on this stamp is from plate 354 of a reprint of *Birds of America* and portrays two

male Louisiana tanagers (now known as western tanagers) in spring plumage at the top of the stamp, as well as two scarlet tanagers—an "old male" in spring plumage and an "old female"—at the bottom of the stamp.

The U.S. Postal Service has twice paid tribute to Audubon himself. The first stamp to honor him was issued in 1940 as part of the Famous Americans series, the second in 1985 as part of the Great Americans series. Two of his other bird portraits were previously featured on three different stamps: "Columbia Jay" appeared on a 1963 issuance, as well as a 1967 airmail stamp; "Long-billed Curlew" was included on the Four Centuries of American Art stamp pane, which was issued in 1998.

Santa Clara, CA
June 27, 2002
Place and Date of Issue

John James Audubon
Artist

Derry Noyes
Designer, Art Director

FACING PAGE: Audubon's "Great blue heron" from Birds of America. *ABOVE: A portrait of Audubon by John Syme. RIGHT: Blue jays from* Birds of America.

Andy Warhol USA 37

Andy Warhol

With his 1962 solo exhibition of the now-famous Campbell's Soup Can paintings at the Ferus Gallery in Los Angeles, Andy Warhol achieved instant notoriety. That same year, the Stable Gallery in New York exhibited, among other works, his Coca-Cola bottles and portraits of Marilyn Monroe and Elvis Presley.

But if you find yourself in Pittsburgh, the city where he was born Andrew Warhola in 1928, stop by The Andy Warhol Museum. That's where you'll find *Self-Portrait, 1964*, the artwork selected by designer Richard Sheaff to grace this new commemorative stamp. Based on a photo-booth photograph, the image—silkscreen ink and synthetic polymer paint on canvas—is one of several versions in varying colors.

As a leading figure in the pop art movement and one of the most influential artists of his time, Warhol gained fame in the advertising world by the mid-1950s with his whimsical and award-winning illustrations. This stamp evokes what are perhaps his best known works: the serial images of celebrities and everyday objects that are virtually synonymous with his name.

Warhol died in New York City on February 22, 1987, but he has remained world famous far longer than the transitory 15 minutes he once predicted for everyone. His career included ventures in design,

photography, film, television, writing, and publishing, and his influence continues in a wide range of creative endeavors throughout contemporary popular culture. For many people, Warhol is inseparable from the art that he created.

But if you're left wondering who Andy Warhol really was, regard his intriguing artwork at the museum that bears his name and consider, for a moment, his own self-description: "If you want to know all about Andy Warhol, just look at the surface: of my paintings and films and me, and there I am. There's nothing behind it."

Pittsburgh, PA
August 9, 2002
Place and Date of Issue

Andy Warhol
Artist

Richard Sheaff
Designer, Art Director

ABOVE: Portrait of Warhol, c. 1967. ABOVE CENTER: A detail of Warhol's Big Campbell's Soup Can, 19¢, 1962. *FACING PAGE: Warhol in 1967. FACING PAGE INSETS: Self-portraits from a photo booth, 1960s.*

© 2001 The Andy Warhol Foundation/ARS, NY.

Teddy Bears

When the U.S. Postal Service issued the 1900s Celebrate the Century stamp pane in 1998, one of the most popular stamps turned out to be the Teddy Bear. This year fans of that stamp are sure to be delighted by these new stamps designed by Margaret Bauer.

But four stamp designs meant that researching the history of these teddy bears would be four times as complex. Needing to enlist an expert consultant, the U.S. Postal Service knew exactly who to call: teddy bear collector, show promoter, and author Linda Mullins.

"I've visited the manufacturers personally so I could use their archives for my research," says Mullins, who recently completed her 18th book on teddy bears. Using encyclopedic knowledge gathered from research trips around the world, Mullins helped to verify the approximate dates for each of these four bears appearing on these stamps, ensuring that they were as accurate as possible.

All four teddy bears featured on these stamps were manufactured in the United States. The Ideal bear dates from circa 1905, the Bruin bear from circa 1907, and the Gund bear from circa 1948. The unlabeled "stick" bear dates from the 1920s. Mass-produced stick bears were characterized by their short arms, thin legs, and upright posture.

"The Postal Service chose the ones with the most history, which are also some of the most appealing," says Mullins, who expects that other teddy bear enthusiasts—known as arctophiles—will be as excited about these stamps as they were about the 1998 stamp. "I have everything that depicted that bear, and I had everyone in the surrounding post offices searching for the various stamp-related items for me," she says with a laugh.

However, Mullins is quick to point out that teddy bears have a serious side. As wonderful symbols of security and comfort, they are often used by police officers and hospital staff to calm children in traumatic situations.

As a result, Mullins says that the greatest reward of her expertise and worldwide travels is seeing the positive effects and truly universal appeal of teddy bears: "My main goal— and I'm so excited it's working—is to make the teddy bear an ambassador of goodwill around the world."

LEFT: A nurse with Operation Desert Storm naps with a teddy bear sent by her family. BELOW: Elizabeth, Duchess of York, c. 1926, with a gift for her daughter—the future Queen Elizabeth II of England.

Atlantic City, NJ
August 15, 2002
Place and Date of Issue

Margaret Bauer
Designer

Derry Noyes
Art Director

The "Hawaiian Missionary" Stamps of 1851-1853

The first official Hawaiian post office was established in December 1850. Postmaster Henry M. Whitney had stamps printed locally in three denominations. Philatelists call these rare stamps "Hawaiian Missionaries" because virtually all were used by Christian missionaries on outbound mail. Only 28 covers with Missionary stamps are known to exist; only the Dawson cover (right) bears the 2¢ stamp. The two 13¢ stamps were unusual as they prepaid postage in two countries–Hawaii and the U.S.

Miss Eliza A. Dawson
Care Jacob H. Dawson
273 Cherry Street
New York

HONOLULU
OCT
4
U.S. Postage Paid

Hawaiian Postage
2
Two Cents

Hawaiian Postage
5
Five Cents

Hawaiian Postage
13
13 Cents

H.I. & U.S. Postage
13
13 Cents

"Hawaiian Missionary" stamp 1851
USA 37

"Hawaiian Missionary" stamp 1851
USA 37

"Hawaiian Missionary" stamp 1851
USA 37

"Hawaiian Missionary" stamp 1852
USA 37

© 2001 USPS

Hawaiian Missionaries

Some stamp projects require a particular knowledge not only of the subject matter, but also of its intended audience. That's why Richard Sheaff of Scottsdale, Arizona, was the perfect choice to serve as designer and art director for the Hawaiian Missionaries souvenir sheet.

"Designing a pane like this one requires me to put on a different hat," he says. "Since I am a philatelist myself, I know that it's important to take a more traditional approach for this kind of project, since this is an extremely classic—and extremely valuable—group of stamps."

The Hawaiian Missionary stamps have teased and intrigued collectors for more than a century with their scarcity. Earning their name because most of them were used on correspondence mailed by Christian missionaries from Hawaii to their families, friends, and business associates, they are now considered among the world's foremost philatelic items. Only 28 covers bearing Missionary stamps are known to exist, and only one surviving cover bears the 2-cent Missionary stamp.

The Hawaiian Missionaries are also an example of philately opening a window to the interesting world of postal history. The first official Hawaiian postal system was created by royal decree in 1850. Henry M. Whitney, the son of missionaries, served as Hawaii's first postmaster and used the press at the government printing office in Honolulu to print stamps.

New York, NY
October 24, 2002
Place and Date of Issue

Richard Sheaff
Designer, Art Director

ABOVE: A portrait of Henry M. Whitney, Hawaii's first postmaster. BACKGROUND: An 1862 engraving of Diamond Head, Honolulu.

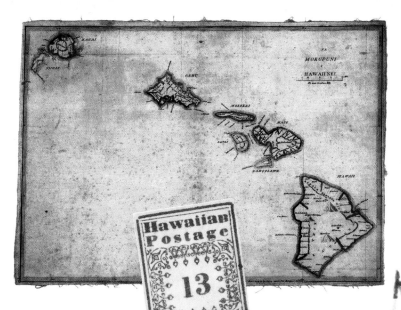

First sold in October 1851, Missionary stamps paid postage on Hawaiian mail to foreign destinations. The 2-cent stamp usually paid the Hawaiian portion of the rate for a newspaper or printed circular. The 5-cent stamp usually paid the Hawaiian portion of letter postage. The typical use of the 13-cent stamp was to prepay all the postage for a letter from Hawaii to the East Coast of the United States by way of San Francisco, applying 5 cents for the Hawaiian charge, 2 cents for the ship captain's fee, and 6 cents for a U.S. letter sent more than 3,000 miles.

Since Hawaii was not annexed by the United States until 1898 and did not become a U.S. territory until 1900, the 13-cent Hawaiian Missionary stamps were unusual because a single stamp prepaid rates in two separate countries: Hawaii and the United States. Of course, this arrangement also caused a few minor problems. U.S. postmasters were confused by the original design for the 13-cent stamp, which read "Hawaiian Postage," so it was redesigned in 1852 to read "H.I. & U.S. Postage."

Richard Sheaff's design incorporates elements that help to tell the engaging story of these deceptively simple stamps. The header image on this new souvenir sheet features a detail of a wood engraving of Diamond Head. According to an archivist at the Bishop Museum in Honolulu, the engraving appeared in an 1862 book entitled *Hawaii: The Past, Present, and Future of Its Island Kingdom.*

Also on the souvenir sheet is a photograph of an envelope sometimes known as the Dawson cover—the only surviving

envelope to bear a 2-cent Hawaiian Missionary stamp. Addressed to Eliza A. Dawson of New York, the envelope bears 2-cent and 5-cent Hawaiian Missionary stamps as well as two 3-cent George Washington stamps. The Dawson cover was found around 1905 among papers stuffed into a furnace; evidence of slight charring is visible on the left edge.

Although they were replaced in 1853 by stamps bearing an image of King Kamehameha III, the Hawaiian Missionary stamps were used as late as 1856 and are still a source of curiosity and interest among philatelists around the world. Ajman, an emirate on the Persian Gulf that is now a member of the United Arab Emirates, issued a stamp in 1965 that featured an image of a 2-cent Missionary stamp alongside that of an early stamp catalog. In 1979 the Ivory Coast issued a stamp featuring a 13-cent Missionary stamp alongside a portrait of Sir Rowland Hill—a British postal reformer credited with the invention of the adhesive postage stamp—and a picture of a locomotive.

Aware of the intense interest that surrounds the Hawaiian Missionaries, Sheaff says that he designed this souvenir sheet with its audience in mind. "It's good to be able to design something for the traditional stamp collector," he says. "These stamps really are examples of classic philately."

ABOVE: A hand-colored 1837 map of Hawaii. BACKGROUND: "Coastal Scene, Hawaii," an 1836 pen-and-ink drawing by French artist Theodore Auguste Fisquet.

Irving Berlin

In 1938, Kate Smith belted out "God Bless America" on her Armistice Day radio broadcast, and the song became an immediate hit. "From the mountains, to the prairies, to the oceans white with foam"—the lyrics are as timeless as the patriotism they express and as recognizable as a national monument.

But ironically, when Irving Berlin wrote the first version of the song in 1918, he dismissed it as too solemn and packed it away. He had been tinkering with it again when Smith needed a patriotic number. Berlin knew that the time was now right, and "God Bless America" became one of his most famous compositions.

This stamp features Berlin's handwritten score of "God Bless America." But is the score really Berlin's? The question vexed stamp researchers, especially because for much of his career Berlin could neither read nor write music—a fact much touted by the press, since it made his songwriting abilities that much more phenomenal. Berlin typically played his songs on a transposing piano, and a musical secretary took down melodies and harmonies in musical notation.

However, one of Berlin's three daughters made a remarkable discovery while going through her father's papers after his death. She found a lead sheet—the vocal melody line and lyrics for a song—for "Soft Lights and Sweet Music," a song Berlin had written in 1932, with his signature and a note that it was the first lead sheet he had written himself. Although Berlin continued to rely on a musical secretary, by the 1930s he had clearly learned to read and write music well enough to write his own simple lead sheet.

When consultation with experts confirmed that this "God Bless America" score, signed by Berlin himself, was probably written in the songwriter's own hand, designer Greg Berger decided to incorporate it into his stamp design. Berger

added both the score and its signature to a colorized black-and-white photograph of Berlin from 1932 by Edward Steichen, one of the most influential photographers of the 20th century.

With more than 1,000 songs to his credit, Berlin—born Israel Beilin in Russia in 1888—knew that universal appeal was the secret to songwriting. During his lifetime he garnered many honors, including the Presidential Medal for Merit, the Presidential Medal of Freedom, and the Congressional Gold Medal. He died at the age of 101 in New York City in 1989, leaving a legacy aptly summed up by Jerome Kern: "Irving Berlin has no place in American music—he *is* American music."

ABOVE: A Hirschfeld caricature captures the essence of Irving Berlin. BELOW: Berlin sings at the dedication of Los Angeles City Hall, 1928. FACING PAGE: Promoting the film Alexander's Ragtime Band *in Boston, 1938.*

New York, NY
September 2002
Place and Date of Issue

Edward Steichen
Photographer

Greg Berger
Designer

Ethel Kessler
Art Director

Madonna and Child

BY JAN GOSSAERT

Each year, the beauty and grace of traditional religious imagery reminds us of the spiritual bonds that connect us during the holiday season—a time for hope, reflection, and family. This new Christmas stamp continues that contemplative spirit with a detail of Jan Gossaert's oil-on-panel painting *Madonna and Child*, circa 1520, from the Charles H. and Mary F. S. Worcester Collection at the Art Institute of Chicago.

Jan Gossaert (circa 1478 to 1532) was a Netherlandish artist credited with being one of the first to bring the innovations of the Italian Renaissance to northern Europe. Specifically, he was a noted draftsman and painter who introduced a greater awareness of anatomy and architectural space to Netherlandish painting. Because Gossaert was a transitional figure in Northern Renaissance art, scholars have had a difficult time classifying him as a member of any single school or style of painting. He has been variously called a Romanist, Antwerp mannerist, and humanist; the debate is ongoing.

Some solemn and austere, others sensitive and highly moving, depictions of the Madonna and Child represent engaging variations on a familiar theme. "We've been doing the Madonna and Child stamps for several years now," says designer and art director Richard Sheaff, who carefully selects the Renaissance paintings that appear on these stamps. With their devoted following and their graceful presentation of fine art, the Christmas stamps themselves have clearly become a tradition in their own right.

Chicago, IL
October 10, 2002
Place and Date of Issue

Jan Gossaert
Artist

Richard Sheaff
Designer, Art Director

FACING PAGE: This painting by Gossaert shows the Madonna and Child with St. Catherine and Mary Magdalene. INSET: A Gossaert diptych from 1517.

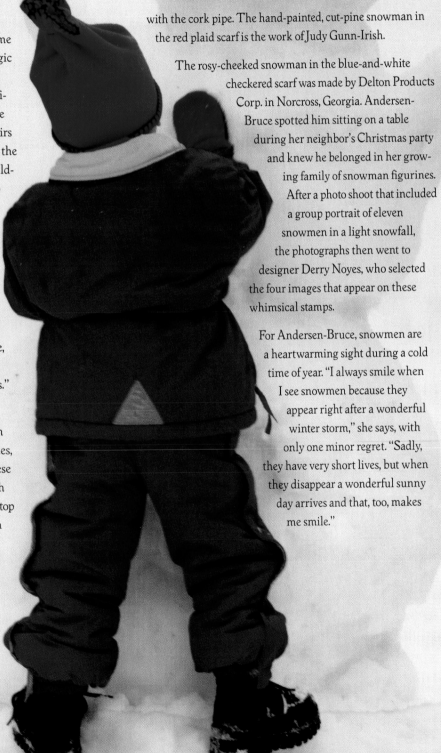

Holiday Snowmen

Popular in folklore, literature, and song, snowmen have come to symbolize the joy and magic of the holiday season. Photographer Sally Andersen-Bruce wasn't specifically looking for snowmen when she visited some of the many fall craft fairs held throughout New England, but the snowmen, pleasant reminders of childhood memories, certainly seemed to be looking for her.

"I decided to attend every craft fair and bazaar in the area where I live," says Andersen-Bruce. "Sometimes I would go to six in one day. I was originally looking for ornaments for another photo project I was working on at the time, but I kept finding wonderful snowmen—so I bought all of my favorites."

Delighted by her new collection, Andersen-Bruce then tracked down the creators of the snowmen figurines, including the four appearing on these stamps. Tommy Simpson made both the Styrofoam snowman wearing a top hat and the combed-wool snowman

with the cork pipe. The hand-painted, cut-pine snowman in the red plaid scarf is the work of Judy Gunn-Irish.

The rosy-cheeked snowman in the blue-and-white checkered scarf was made by Delton Products Corp. in Norcross, Georgia. Andersen-Bruce spotted him sitting on a table during her neighbor's Christmas party and knew he belonged in her growing family of snowman figurines. After a photo shoot that included a group portrait of eleven snowmen in a light snowfall, the photographs then went to designer Derry Noyes, who selected the four images that appear on these whimsical stamps.

For Andersen-Bruce, snowmen are a heartwarming sight during a cold time of year. "I always smile when I see snowmen because they appear right after a wonderful winter storm," she says, with only one minor regret. "Sadly, they have very short lives, but when they disappear a wonderful sunny day arrives and that, too, makes me smile."

Chicago, IL
October 2002
Place and Date of Issue

Sally Andersen-Bruce
Photographer

Derry Noyes
Designer, Art Director

Duke Kahanamoku

He was a living legend: champion swimmer, world-famous surfer, and a symbol of Hawaiian hospitality and goodwill. For decades, visiting celebrities, foreign royalty, and tourists alike all hoped to meet Duke Kahanamoku—or, at the very least, to catch a glimpse of him on the beach. Those fortunate to encounter "the Duke" recall not only the great strength and athletic prowess that made him famous, but also the charm, generosity, and quiet wisdom that endeared him to the world.

Kahanamoku competed on the U.S. team in several Olympic Games from 1912 to 1932, bringing home a number of medals, breaking freestyle records, and impressing even his opponents with his good sportsmanship. Known as the father of modern surfing, Kahanamoku is also credited with popularizing the Polynesian sport by surfing throughout the world, especially on visits to Australia and the East Coast of the United States.

Remembered for his grace and hospitality, Duke Kahanamoku was, in the words of stamp designer Carl T. Herrman, "the personification of the *aloha* spirit of Hawaii." Herrman has designed more than 250 commemorative stamps, but the Duke Kahanamoku stamp is special for him: It honors one of his heroes.

"We named our boards for Hawaiian gods and dreamed of someday surfing the islands," recalls Herrman, who was an ocean lifeguard at Tobay Beach in Long Island, New York, during the late 1950s and early 1960s. He points out that surfing-related projects have long been central to his career: "I used to be the East Coast rep for *Surfer* magazine and editor of *Surfing East*, which was the first East Coast magazine about surfing." He has high praise for Michael J. Deas, who painted the stamp art. "Michael did a fabulous job," he says, describing the artist as an intense researcher who is relentless in his pursuit of authenticity.

Honolulu, HI
August 24, 2002
Place and Date of Issue

Michael J. Deas
Artist

Carl T. Herrman
Designer, Art Director

Herrman now lives in Carlsbad, California, where he can be seen driving to the beaches near his home in his restored red Citroën. "My love of surfing," he says, "continues stronger than ever."

LEFT: *With his surfboard, c. 1930.* ABOVE: *Memorabilia from a celebrated life.* FACING PAGE: *Kahanamoku in 1928.*

Photo Credits

Lunar New Year: Year of the Horse

Pages 8–9

©Giraudon/Art Resource, New York

Black Heritage: Langston Hughes

Page 10

Reprinted courtesy of National Portrait Gallery, Smithsonian Institution; Gift of W. Tjark Reiss, in memory of his father, Winold Reiss

Page 11

(top) Photograph by Carl Van Vechten. Used by permission of the Van Vechten Trust.

(center) Reproduced by permission of Alfred A. Knopf Publishers, Inc.

Winter Sports

Page 12

(top) ©Duomo/CORBIS

(middle) ©Getty Images/Elsa Hasch

(bottom) ©Getty Images/Brian Bahr

Pages 12–13

©Getty Images/Mike Powell

Greetings From America

Pages 14–15

(background) ©D. Boone/CORBIS

Page 15

(inset) ©Lake County Museum/CORBIS

Pages 16–17

©Frank Kuchirchuk/Superstock

Page 16

(bottom) ©Lake County Museum/CORBIS

Page 17

(top) ©Lake County Museum/CORBIS

(second from top) ©Lake County Museum/CORBIS

(bottom) ©Lake County Museum/CORBIS

Harry Houdini

Page 18–19

(all) Courtesy Library of Congress

Happy Birthday

Pages 20–21

(background) ©Philip James Corwin/CORBIS

Page 21

(top right) ©Bill Schild/CORBIS

(bottom left) ©Joe Atlas/Brand X Pictures/PictureQuest

Neuter or Spay

Pages 22–23

(all) ©2001 U.S. Postal Service

Literary Arts: Ogden Nash

Page 24

(top) Drawing provided by Frances R. Smith

(center) Photograph provided by Frances R. Smith

(bottom) Julian DeMiskey/*The New Yorker*, The Condé Nast Publications Inc.

Page 25

©Bettman/CORBIS

Masters of American Photography

Page 26

(top center) Title: James VanDerZee, Self-Portrait, 1918 Photographer: James VanDerZee ©Donna Mussenden VanDerZee

(bottom center) Collection Center for Creative Photography reproduced with permission of the Georgia O'Keeffe Foundation

Pages 26–27

(background) W. Eugene Smith Archive, Center for Creative Photography, The University of Arizona, Tucson

Page 28

©1950, Nancy Newhall, ©2002, The Estate of Beaumont Newhall and Nancy Newhall. Courtesy of Scheinbaum and Russek Ltd., Santa Fe, NM.

Page 29

(top left) Courtesy of George Eastman House

(top center) ©1978 The Imogen Cunningham Trust

(top right) ©Bettman/CORBIS

(bottom left) Courtesy of George Eastman House

(bottom center) Courtesy Library of Congress

(bottom right) ©The Dorothea Lange Collection, Oakland Museum of California, City of Oakland. Gift of Paul S. Taylor.

United States Military Academy

Page 30

(top left) ©U.S. Army Photo

(center) ©2001 U.S. Postal Service

(bottom right) ©U.S. Army Photo

Page 31

©U.S. Army Photo

Legends of Hollywood: Cary Grant

Page 32

(lower left) Courtesy of Photofest

(upper right) ©Bettman/CORBIS

Page 33

Courtesy of Photofest

Mentoring a Child

Page 34

(top center) ©Brendan Mattingly

(center left) ©Brendan Mattingly

(center right) ©Steve Chenn/CORBIS

Page 35

©Monkmeyer, Rex Intstock/Stock Connection/PictureQuest

Nature of America: Longleaf Pine Forest

Pages 36–37

©Fred Whitehead/Animals Animals

Page 37

(upper left) ©Robert Winslow/ Animals Animals

(center left) ©Joe McDonald/Animals Animals

(bottom) ©David Shirk/Animals Animals

P h o t o   C r e d i t s

Women in Journalism

Page 38

(background) Courtesy Library of Congress

(bottom inset) General Research Division, The New York Public Library, Astor, Lenox and Tilden Foundation.

Page 39

(background) Courtesy of Ida M. Tarbell Collection, Pelletier Library, Allegheny College, Meadville, Pa.

(bottom inset) From Pennsylvania Historical & Museum Commission, Drake Well Museum Collection, Titusville, PA

Page 40

(background) ©Hulton-Deutsch Collection/CORBIS

(bottom inset) Courtesy of the Center for American History, The University of Texas at Austin.

Page 41

(background) ©1982, *The Washington Post* Photo by Joel Richardson. Reprinted with Permission.

(bottom inset) Reproduced with permission of the *Chicago Defender*.

American Bats

Page 42

(center) ©Merlin D. Tuttle, Bat Conservation International

(top right) ©Joe McDonald/CORBIS

Page 43

©Merlin D. Tuttle, Bat Conservation International

American Treasures: John James Audubon

Page 44

Courtesy Library of Congress

Page 45

(top) White House Collection, ©White House Historical Association

(bottom right) Courtesy of Bridgeman Art Library/Natural History Museum, London, UK

Andy Warhol

Page 46

(background) ©Billy Name, courtesy Kevin Kushel, Ovoworks

(insets) The Andy Warhol Museum, Pittsburgh, Founding Collection ©2002 The Andy Warhol Foundation for the Visual Arts/ARS, NY. Contribution The Andy Warhol Foundation for the Visual Arts, Inc.

Page 47

(top right) ©Hulton-Deutsch Collection/CORBIS

(center) The Menil Collection, Houston. ©2002 Andy Warhol Foundation/ ARS, NY/™ licensed by Campbell's Soup Co. All Rights Reserved.

Teddy Bears

Page 48

(left) ©David Turnley/CORBIS

(right) ©Hulton-Deutsch Collection/CORBIS

Page 49

©2001 U.S. Postal Service

Hawaiian Missionaries

Pages 50–51

(background) Bishop Museum

Page 51

(center) Taber, Bishop Museum

Page 52

(top) Courtesy Library of Congress

(inset stamps) Siegel Auction Galleries Inc.

Pages 52–53

(background) Bishop Museum

Irving Berlin

Page 54

(background) Photo courtesy The Irving Berlin Music Company

(top inset) Courtesy of The Irving Berlin Music Company

(lower inset) Courtesy of The Irving Berlin Music Company

Page 55

(top) ©Al Hirschfeld, art reproduced by special arrangement with Hirschfeld's exclusive representative, The Margo Feiden Galleries Ltd., New York.

(bottom) ©Bettman/CORBIS

Christmas: *Madonna and Child* **by Jan Gossaert**

Pages 56–57

(background) Courtesy of Bridgeman Art Library/Hamburg Kunsthalle, Hamburg, Germany

Page 57

(inset) ©Reunion des Musées Nationaux/Art Resource, New York

Holiday Snowmen

Page 58

©2001 U.S. Postal Service

Page 59

©Chris Carroll/CORBIS

Duke Kahanamoku

Duke Kahanamoku's likeness used with permission of Malama Pono, Ltd., a California corporation, owner of all commercial rights of exploitation to Duke Kahanamoku's name and likeness. All rights reserved.

Page 60

(left) Tai Sing Loo, Provided by Bishop Museum.

(top right) Provided by Bishop Museum.

(center right) Provided by Hawaiian Collection, Hamilton Library, University of Hawaii at Manoa.

Page 61

Courtesy Library of Congress.

A c k n o w l e d g m e n t s

These stamps and this stamp-collecting book were produced by Government Relations and Public Policy, Stamp Services, and the United States Postal Service.

John E. Potter
Postmaster General,
Chief Executive Officer

Deborah K. Willhite
Senior Vice President,
Government Relations and Public Policy

Catherine Caggiano
Executive Director,
Stamp Services

Special thanks are extended to the following individuals for their contributions to the production of this book:

UNITED STATES POSTAL SERVICE

Terrence W. McCaffrey
Manager, Stamp Development

Kelly L. Spinks
Project Manager

HARPERCOLLINS PUBLISHERS

Megan Newman
Editorial Director,
HarperResource

Greg Chaput
Associate Editor,
HarperResource

Lucy Albanese
Design Director,
General Books Group

NIGHT & DAY DESIGN

Timothy Shaner
Art Director, Designer

PHOTOASSIST, INC.

Jeff Sypeck
Copywriter

Anne Pietromica
Text Research

Mike Owens
Photo Editor

Kirsty McGuire
Rights and Permissions

THE CITIZENS' STAMP ADVISORY COMMITTEE

Dr. Virginia M. Noelke
Cary R. Brick
Michael R. Brock
Meredith J. Davis
David L. Eynon
Jean Picker Firstenberg
Sylvia Harris
I. Michael Heyman
John M. Hotchner
Dr. C. Douglas Lewis
Karl Malden
Dr. Philip B. Meggs
Richard F. Phelps
Ronald A. Robinson
John Sawyer III